MW00422713

"Scott has an amazing way of discussing a wide variety of sales-related subjects and boiling them down into *easily actionable strategies and tasks.* Whether you are just starting in the business or have been in direct or vendor sales for 25 years, this book will help you clarify how to maximize your efforts."
- *Chris Enbom, CLFP*
CEO, Allegiant Partners Incorporated

"Whether by sheer attrition or on purpose, new blood will be entering the equipment leasing and finance industry in the very near future. How will we provide them sales training in our industry? What tools can we give them? There hasn't been a sales guide of sorts for our industry since Bill Granieri, until now! Scott's book, Call to Action, may well be the best investment any manager or executive can make in his sales staff and company. Scott is extraordinarily efficient in dispensing usable knowledge in a concise, easily understood manner delivered in short modules complete with a call to action for each concept. I have been in this industry for 20+ years and while reading Call to Action, I found myself pondering his ideas multiple times during the process. If I can still learn something about our industry, others can too. Get this book for your teams!"
- *Bob Rinaldi*
CEO, Commercial Industrial Finance

"Scott has done a tremendous job at putting many ideas together in one book for the equipment leasing business. For the seasoned professional or one just starting, the insights to the sales process are proven and offer a strong foundation for success. From beginning to end, it gives great guidance from a true expert."

- *Pete Sawyer, CLFP*
President, Sun South Equipment Leasing, Inc.

"Scott Wheeler condenses his 35 years of sales and prospecting expertise into an easy to read book. Any professional in the equipment financing or leasing industry who is looking to "freshen up" their skills can learn from this well thought out and well-structured manuscript. Scott's examples clearly highlight real life situations that have occurred in our industry. You can learn a lot by following his roadmap to success, and learning from the experiences of others. It's an easy read, and anyone following the steps laid out by Scott can expect to see tangible results."

- *Bruce Winter, CLFP*
President, FSG Capital

Call to Action

For Commercial Equipment Leasing and Finance Professionals

Scott A. Wheeler
CLFP

ISBN: 1508750378
ISBN-13: 978-1508750376
Library of Congress Control Number: 2015910178
CreateSpace Independent Publishing Platform
Fallston, Maryland

Table of Contents

Table of Contents

Table of Contents

Preface

Much has changed since I began my career in the commercial equipment leasing and finance industry in the early 1980's. Automation has obviously evolved at great speed, leading to many efficiencies and innovative solutions. As the industry has matured, so have the end-users and vendors that are far more educated now than ever before about leasing and finance services. However, many constants remain: hardworking professionals who focus on superior customer service continue to thrive; professionals who embrace change, innovation and creativity continue to lead the industry; and organizations that originate and manage strong, well-performing assets continue to outperform the competition.

This book serves as a guide to success. I suggest you read the book not in one sitting but rather on a periodic basis to reinforce learning and self-improvement. The book was written as a reference for C-level executives, managers, and sales professionals who need a "Call to Action." I have compiled my favorite "Weekly Sales Tips" into a one-volume, easy-to-use collection of observations, experiences, and anecdotes. As with my weekly tips, the book prompts you to think beyond the established ideas, to re-evaluate your present practices, and to question past experiences.

Each topic contains "Call to Action" exercises that are meant to encourage activities, all of which can be revisited on a regular basis. You will find different benefits based upon your own current strengths, weaknesses, and challenges. I encourage sales teams to read and work through the exercises together. Disagreement, whether with me or one another, is part of the learning process – as we all know by our own personal experiences, there is no one way to be successful in the commercial equipment leasing and finance industry. With that said, the ideas presented in this book have been tried by others in the industry with proven success. Sales professionals have internalized the tips provided and significantly improved their personal results.

This book is "A Call to Action." It is a call to all professionals to succeed in a vibrant industry – an industry that offers exciting opportunity for those with an entrepreneurial spirit. It is a call to all who take the information in this book to formulate personal successes. It is a call to all who are willing to properly manage their time and accomplishments so that the next cold call becomes the next warm handshake and mutually beneficial relationship.

Chapter 1

**Developing New Clients
by
Prospecting & Cold Calling**

Priority #1

The primary responsibility of every leasing and finance originator is to develop new clients. Every client begins as a prospect. In order to bring real value to an organization, the originator must engage in continuous efforts of contacting and developing his prospect list into future customers. Prospecting is a full-time, daily proposition. **The most successful originators make prospecting their number one priority.**

Transactions appear from the most unlikely places. Strong originators are opportunists at heart, working 24/7 to find new business opportunities. It's the last cold call of the day, the casual lunch meeting, the newspaper article, the roadside billboard, or the business name attached to a truck that inspires the best originators to reach out and offer services to new clients. Nothing happens until we engage with the people who are right in front us every day.

One of the most common questions asked by originators is: *"How much time do I need to set aside for prospecting for new business?"*

This primary question leads to additional investigation:

- How satisfied are you with your current production?
- How satisfied are you with your current income?
- How satisfied are you with your current backlog?

If you are 100% satisfied with the results, you may be able to get away with 20% of your time spent prospecting for new business, new relationships, and new transactions. If you are not 100% satisfied with the results, then you need to immediately increase prospecting time by 10% from its current pace (from

30% to 40%, or 55% to 65%). If your results are below expectations, or stated goals, then prospecting may need to be increased to nearly 100% of your time, until the situation changes. You hold the various keys to your own success, and the keys usually start with letting more contacts, vendors, and end-users know that you exist. Success is derived from strong, targeted prospecting efforts.

Increased Prospecting Efforts
Equal Greater Results

"Priority #1"
Call to Action Questions:

1) How much time are you currently spending prospecting for new clients?

2) Should you be spending additional time prospecting for new clients? What is holding you back?

3) Dissect your last ten transactions. Where did they originate?

4) Do you develop new prospects 24/7 outside of the work environment? Why? Or why not?

5) Have your prospecting efforts increased or decreased recently? Why?

Offering Solutions

Leasing and finance originators often forget the power of their products. Successful originators sell "Cash Flow" solutions to businesses seeking to expand their capabilities, to improve efficiency, and to reach new levels of competitiveness. Originators need to confidently flaunt, explain, and reveal the true value of their products and personal services.

Many originators work diligently to find a good prospect. They make several calls before identifying the correct contact within a prospective company. Unfortunately, when they have the opportunity to introduce themselves and their products, they turn the opportunity into a dead end question: *"Do you have any financing or leasing needs today?"* The answer is usually *"no."* There the conversation ends. Successful originators inform the client as to how their financing options can both maximize acquisition potential and, at the same time, minimize cash flow requirements.

Prospecting in any service business is all about planting seeds, encouraging prospects to think about their challenges, and presenting meaningful solutions.

When prospecting for new business, explain the benefits of your products. Offer examples of how your products have helped other clients acquire needed equipment, increase efficiency, and expand profitability. Top producers understand the impact of their products and do not hesitate to fully explain how equipment leasing and financing is a powerful solution for businesses looking to grow and prosper.

Flaunt the Impact of Your Products

"Offering Solutions"
Call to Action Questions

1) Are you offering real solutions to your prospects?

2) Do you provide examples of how your products and services have helped other clients? What are those examples?

3) Are you flaunting your strengths when making prospecting calls?

4) Do you perceive yourself as a sales representative, or an advisor who provides meaningful solutions?

5) Do you present yourself and your products and services with enthusiasm and optimism?

Qualifying Prospects

Strong leasing and finance originators always have a "Hot List" of new prospects. The process includes probing research and, more importantly, strong listening skills. Identifying and qualifying a strong "Hot List" is essential to success.

Strong originators are capable of digesting both positive and negative information.

There is no shame in properly qualifying a prospect and making an intellectual decision that the lead is not a proper fit. The best relationships are formed when leads are elevated to priority status based upon total understanding. The only negative outcome is when prospects are not properly vetted and wither away because of lack of attention.

You can develop your "Hot List" by consistently answering the following questions:

- Who are your top (five, ten, twenty, etc.) prospects?
- What is the industry in which each prospect participates?
- What do you know about each prospect?
- What is its financial strength?
- How long have you been pursuing each prospect?
- Why do you consider each prospect a strong potential client?
- Does this prospect align with your capabilities?

As a strong originator, you must ask the tough questions and fully qualify your "Hot List" on a continuous basis.

A Qualified Prospect is Golden

"Qualifying Prospects"
Call to Action Questions:

1) Are you listening to your prospects?

2) Do you have a "Hot List" of top prospects?

3) How well do you know your "Hot List"?

4) How has your "Hot List" changed in the last 30 or 60 days?

5) Are you consistently and constantly qualifying your prospects?

6) Do you use a ranking system for prospects and customers?

Know the Competition

Successful commercial equipment leasing and finance originators know who and what they are competing against. It's not enough for originators to know their products well; originators are required to know how their products and services fit into the broader markets among all competitors.

Top producers don't fear competition; they embrace the opportunity to outperform their competition.

A veteran originator was faced with a competitor that had beaten her on a fairly large relationship. After more investigation and verification, the originator found that this particular competitor had become slightly more aggressive by developing new programs designed specifically for this niche market. The originator and her products could rightfully compete against this adversary. The verified information allowed the originator to re-engage in the market from a position of knowledge and confidence, thus encouraging the veteran to sell and market herself more aggressively. She quickly won several opportunities where she was in direct competition with the same competitor. By fully understanding both the competitor and various emerging forces in the market, the originator was forced to become more aggressive, flaunt her strengths, and serve her clients with superior services.

None of your competitors are able to do it all. Competition should encourage you to offer superior services and grow as a professional.

Knowledge is Power

"Know the Competition"
Call to Action Questions:

1) Who are your top five competitors?

2) What are their strengths?

3) What are their weaknesses?

4) Where do you fit in the market? And why?

5) How do you compete against your top competitors?

6) Give examples of how you have adapted to competition in the past and become a better competitor in the market.

Simple, Concise & Powerful

The commercial equipment finance and leasing business is not complicated. Top producers use simple concepts to sell their products to a wide range of prospects on a continuous basis.

"Why should a potential client use YOU instead of a competitor?"

When an industry veteran was asked the "WHY" question, he quickly launched into a twenty minute dissertation that was informative, but totally exhausting. When I asked if he could summarize his comments into two or three sentences, he continued for another ten minutes. Basically, this industry veteran was Superman – he wasn't completely sure how he helped his customers, but he was completely positive that within his toolbox there was a solution to every financial need a customer could possibly require.

LESS can be more powerful and definitely more meaningful.

A great exercise is to find a ten-year-old and explain to them *what you do for a living and why your services are needed.* After you are finished – ask your son/daughter/niece or nephew to tell you what they have learned. Kids are brutally honest and their attention spans are longer than most of your potential clients.

The strongest originators know who they are in the industry. They are able to offer superior services and connect with their potential clients. Most importantly, they are able to answer questions with simple, concise, and powerful statements.

Keep it Simple

Simple, Concise & Powerful
<u>Call to Action Questions:</u>

1) Could you explain your business to a
   ten-year-old?

2) Why should a client use your services?
   (in 30 words or less)

3) Do you quickly connect to your customers?

4) Give an example of how you have
   successfully simplified a complex concept
   into an easy to understand explanation.

5) Do you ever find yourself speaking more
   than listening?

Referrals

The fastest means to improved production is to have your existing clients and business partners provide referrals. Referrals can come in many forms including:

- Vendors referring end-users.
- End-users referring vendors.
- A vendor sales rep. referring another sales rep. within his company.
- An end-user contact referring a colleague in a different department.
- A client referring a friend.
- An accountant or attorney referring his best client.
- A banker referring his commercial customers.

Success is often defined by the strength of your network and by the success of your referrals.

The strongest originators ask for new referrals on a daily basis. Vendors, end-users, and other sources are usually more than willing to help originators broaden their contacts and web of referrals when asked. If you want stronger transactions, you need to confidently ask for them. If you want larger transactions, you need to confidently ask for them. If you want more referrals, you need to ask for them.

Originators Get What They Ask For

"Referrals"
Call to Action Questions:

1) Do you ask for referrals on a regular basis
   a. From existing clients?
   b. From vendors?
   c. From all contacts you speak with on a daily basis?

2) Provide an example of how a referral developed into a key account.

3) What actions need to be taken to increase referrals?

4) When funding a transaction do you make a special effort to thank your clients for the business and ask for a referral?

5) What services do you offer that earn you additional referrals on a consistent basis?

Blitz

Leasing and finance originators need to spend time "blitzing" their database. I generally recommend methodical, focused efforts to gain greater penetration into vendors and end-users. However, a good calling blitz is an effective means of getting your name out to the market. A blitzing effort is fast and hard-hitting with real results. I usually define a blitz as an initiative with double the amount of calls typically made in a given period. There should be a consistent message presented concisely and with enthusiasm.

The purpose of having a calling blitz is not simply to make more calls, but rather to develop results.

Enthusiasm is essential. Ranking results (1, 2, 3 or A, B, C) and having a consistent follow-up plan of action for each group is critical for success. The purpose of a strong blitzing initiative is to create a new group of HOT prospects which otherwise would have never been discovered. Blitzes can be even more productive when several sales reps. join forces to leverage their efforts by sharing gathered information, proud successes, and even disastrous failures. A blitz competition is a great means of re-energizing an office: who can contact the most companies, who can find the best potential new clients, or who can generate the most new applications. A blitz can last a few hours, or perhaps a day or two, but not much longer – otherwise, it just becomes routine calling with many dials and few results.

Originators who are committed to building their business make the time to blitz their database on a regular basis.

Penetrate the Defensive Line with a Strong Blitz

> ## *"Blitz"*
> ## <u>*Call to Action Questions:*</u>
>
> 1) When was the last time you blitzed your database?
>
> 2) What was the objective of the blitz?
>
> 3) Was the blitz productive?
>
> 4) How did you rank or quantify your results?
>
> 5) What list or segment of your database will you blitz next?

Overcoming Objections

Successful commercial leasing and finance originators have concise rebuttals to convert objections into opportunities. Most objections fall into one of the following six categories:

- We (our customers) pay cash for all acquisitions.
- We are not looking at any acquisitions.
- Rates are too high.
- We always use our bank for equipment acquisitions.
- We already have a leasing/finance partner.
- We have not leased for years.

Each of these objections is basically a smoke screen.

The originator who doesn't push through these objections is just conducting a superficial cold calling exercise. Top producers anticipate these objections and are able to turn them into purposeful conversations. For example, as a rebuttal to a customer who suggests they always pay cash, you may consider the following:

"Mr. Customer, I often help clients who originally intend to pay cash for their equipment. However, once they review my programs and low monthly payments, they decide to conserve their cash and take advantage of my very competitive programs. What equipment projects are you considering? I am delighted to provide you with the necessary capital to help your business grow and prosper."

You should speak from the heart and push every conversation forward.

Convert Objections into Opportunities

"Overcoming Objections"
Call to Action Questions:

1) What objections do you encounter most often?

2) What is your typical response to these objections?

3) Are you converting objections into opportunities?

4) Do you accept objections too easily and move on – or do you use objections to probe further?

5) Do you provide examples of how you have helped other clients with the same objections?

Chapter 2

Strong Relationships

Relationships are Earned

Commercial equipment leasing and finance originators have the task of developing relationships that are capable of generating strong transactions. The best vendor and end-user relationships are earned through diligent efforts.

Transactions that are easily generated are usually less than desirable. End-users who seek out funding sources through internet searches often create reason for concern. Vendors who throw open their doors to originators and are willing to work with a new financial partner each week or month should be treated with similar caution. However, end-users and vendors who question your value usually develop into your most valuable clients.

Veteran originators know relationships worth having are relationships worth earning.

One of the most effective prospecting questions to ask is: *"How can I earn your business?"* Strong originators embrace the challenge of working on relationships and transactions that require expertise and value. The best relationships are multidimensional and continuously changing, thereby allowing the originator to best serve the needs of his clients.

The key to a strong relationship with any vendor or end-user is a thorough understanding of the customer's needs and wants. You want to know your customer's challenges, successes, and failures and why the customer has chosen you as its financial partner.

Success Comes from Earning
Every Relationship

"Relationships Are Earned"
<u>*Call to Action Questions:*</u>

1) Have your current relationships been earned over time?

2) Have you fallen into the trap of spending valuable time with casual relationships that never produce real results?

3) Do you chase transactions or cultivate long-term relationships?

4) Do you ask the tough questions upfront to pre-qualify your relationships?

5) Are you wary of potential clients that suddenly appear out of thin air?

A Financial Partner

Vendors and end-users seek strong financial partners to help them navigate the ever-changing economy. There are always new opportunities for aggressive originators willing to invest in meaningful business partnerships.

An effective "Financial Partner" requires more expertise and knowledge than a "Sales Representative."

Strong financial partners are an integral part of a vendor's selling process. A strong vendor relationship includes education, support, and communication. Vendors want partners who are involved in all stages of the sales cycle and can expedite the process. A financial partner gets involved, takes control, and delivers results for his primary vendors.

Strong financial partners think beyond one transaction and act beyond an "application only" mentality. They prepare end-users for the underwriting process and build credit files for on-going financial needs. Financial partners take the time to understand the needs and wants of end-users and, more specifically, advise end-users based upon their financial strengths. Choosing their clients carefully, financial partners provide meaningful advice and multidimensional solutions.

Strong originators are continuously building new financial partnerships and offering superior services to their preferred clients.

Start New Partnerships

> ### *"A Financial Partner"*
> ### <u>*Call to Action Questions:*</u>
>
> 1) Do you consider yourself a sales rep. or a financial partner?
>
> 2) Do you become part of the process?
>
> 3) Do your clients call you for financial advice?
>
> 4) Do you help to educate your clients about the benefits of your services?
>
> 5) Do you have a network of complementary services or professionals that you refer to your top clients?

Four Stages of a Vendor Relationship

As with any relationship, the interaction between originators and equipment vendors evolves during the course of many different stages. It is important for an originator to understand the specific stage of the relationship in which she is currently involved. It is equally as important to realize there are opportunities (applications) to be realized at each stage. The opportunities increase in numbers and quality as an originator/vendor relationship progresses through each stage. (Note: One transaction from a vendor does not constitute a strong established relationship.)

Stage 1
Introduction

The first stage of any relationship is getting to know one another. The process is a two-way street. The vendor needs to know the originator's capabilities and conversely, the originator should be investigating the vendor. The introduction stage starts from the very first call. It can occur over just a few calls, multiple meetings/calls, or even several transactions (timing between a few days to a few months). This is an investigative process whereby both parties are trying to determine whether or not the relationship is a viable match.

In order to have success in Stage 1, the originator must be proactive and investigative. Questions must be probing, and the originator should listen intently to the answers to sincerely determine whether or not there is a match.

Stage 2
Delivery

The second stage of the relationship is the first real test of compatibility. During this stage transactions start to flow (meaning several transactions over a relatively short period). The vendor and originator both want results (approvals and fundings). The originator is looking for quality transactions that meet the credit criteria and are winnable within the originator's structure and pricing capabilities. The vendor is looking for quality, superior service, competitive programs, and prompt funding capabilities.

Stage 3
Commitment

After much diligence on the part of both the vendor and the originator, a real commitment develops. Trust is confirmed between both parties. The vendor and the originator work as a team to enhance both parties' ability to increase sales and bottom line profits. There is a free flow of information between the originator and the vendor. The vendor wants to provide appropriate information to protect the risk of the originator; the originator offers superior service, pricing, and structures that allow the vendor to be most competitive in the market. In order to reach the commitment stage, both parties must truly understand the other's business and be invested in the success of the total relationship. The originator is a primary stakeholder in the vendor's supply chain and, conversely, is treated as such.

The third stage of a vendor relationship is a win-win proposition for all parties. It is at this stage of development when an originator can claim she has a meaningful vendor relationship.

Stage 4
Sustainability

Long-term sustainability is, often times, the most difficult stage of a relationship. Because of constant changes by forces from within the relationship and without (often out of one's control), vendor relationships are often hard to maintain. The strongest originator/vendor relationships are sustained by furthering consistent efforts.

The originator must never take a committed vendor relationship for granted. It is an ongoing process to maintain and grow an existing vendor relationship. As with any relationship,
stumbles may occur along the way. A committed originator will embrace the challenges as opportunities to redefine her value. By navigating through the challenges the originator will enhance the entire relationship.

Rank Your Vendor Relationships by Stage

"Four Stages of a Vendor Relationship"
<u>*Call to Action Questions:*</u>

1) Rank your top vendor relationships by their
    current stage.

2) What "Must be True" to progress each
    relationship to the next stage?

3) How can you block your competitors from
    invading your vendor relationships?

4) How can you protect a relationship from
    falling back into a previous stage? And
    keep relationships moving forward?

5) What are you doing to sustain your
    best relationships?

Building Trust

Trust (noun): *reliance on the integrity, strength, ability, surety of a person or thing; confidence*

Leasing and finance originators are selling an intangible product. Therefore, the essential factor in every sale is the originator's ability to build trust between the client and himself. Extensive knowledge in all aspects of the leasing and finance process helps to develop a position of strength and builds trust with individual clients. Equally as important is the ability to recognize limitations. There is no shame in admitting you don't know everything, but that you will find an answer to a specific challenge and report back to the client in a timely manner.

Facts, honesty, integrity, and results are essential factors in building trust.

Originators who deliver on their promises will always come out ahead. Originators who are upfront about their capabilities are able to build long lasting relationships with vendors and end-users that will be best served by their services and products.

Vendors and end-users buy from you, the originator, and your ability to provide a reasonable solution to their financial needs. The first step in building trust is to allow the customer to learn who you really are and what your real capabilities are in the market. Trust is established through communication, actions, and unbroken promises.

Trust is Personal

"Building Trust"
Call to Action Questions:

1) Do you under promise and over deliver?

2) Do you trust your clients? Why or why not?

3) Do you listen to your clients to help build trust?

4) Are you respectful of your client's time and are they respectful of your time?

5) Describe relationships you have built based upon total trust and that are mutually beneficial to all parties.

Front Line

Strong originators in the commercial equipment leasing and finance industry know the importance of standing on the front line. They have a passion for total engagement in the market and building new relationships with potential clients. A long productive day of prospecting calls or face-to-face meetings provides personal satisfaction for top originators.

You will expand your position in the market by working in a proactive manner.

At times, an originator will retreat to meet with colleagues, plan, and re-energize. However, the strongest originators quickly return to the marketing/sales front line because they know the execution of any marketing plan is best conducted by communicating directly with vendors and end-users, standing in front of decision makers, and participating in the real action. The commercial equipment leasing and finance industry is highly competitive, and successful originators protect their position in the market by using their marketing time wisely.

Aggressive, consistent marketing and sales processes will allow you to gather vital marketing intelligence, establish relationships, consummate more transactions, and build market penetration. Your opportunities are limitless when you spend valuable time on the front line with "real" decision makers.

Successful Originators Stretch
Every Day

"Front Line"
Call to Action Questions:

1) Describe a strong and satisfactory day of prospecting.

2) Give an example of a small relationship that developed into a significant long-term relationship.

3) How do you place limitations on yourself?

4) How can you avoid self-imposed limitations?

5) Do you quickly return to the "front line" after a distraction?

6) Do you push yourself to give 100% every day? What are the results?

Listen Carefully

Leasing and finance originators often want to demonstrate how knowledgeable they are about their products and will dominate discussions detailing their superior services. However, vendors or end-users are typically more concerned about expressing their specific needs and challenges rather than hearing about an originator's supernatural capabilities. Originators who listen more than they speak build stronger relationships.

In order to outperform your competition, you need to be well-versed on all aspects of the leasing process and prepared to explain the process in detail when necessary. However, it is not necessary for you to relay all of your knowledge to every client. Unnecessary information can confuse and complicate transactions. The responsibility of the leasing and finance originator is to simplify the process by offering meaningful solutions and information that will allow the process to progress toward funding. Different clients are seeking different information. It is your responsibility to adjust to each situation.

When your customer is speaking, listen.

Whenever you interrupt a customer to inject your thoughts, you are actually building barriers in the relationship. By listening more and speaking less, the "real" needs of the vendors and end-users are better served.

Listen Intently

"Listen Carefully"
<u>*Call to Action Questions:*</u>

1) Who did most of the talking on your last call – you or the client?

2) Do you oversell your products?

3) Do you make an effort to listen before you speak?

4) Do you ask opened ended questions and allow your clients sufficient time to respond?

Leveraging Relationships

Originators often spend their time looking for new relationships when there is plenty of untapped business within their established network of vendors and end-users.

You need to leverage every relationship and transaction to maximize your effectiveness in the market.

An originator once explained how an existing end-user acquired a type of equipment he had never provided funding for in the past. The transaction proceeded smoothly, and the originator reached out to the "new" vendor, enthusiastically establishing a new vendor relationship. This was a great first step. However, many other potential opportunities now presented themselves:

- Could other existing clients, in the originator's niche market, also need this new equipment?
- Were other vendors considered when the existing customer acquired the equipment?
- What other industries does this new vendor sell equipment to?
- How could this originator exploit this one transaction into new opportunities and increased income?

Endless possibilities exist when originators leverage every relationship and every situation into new opportunities. In order to be a top producer, you must leverage relationships and consistently ask for business. Vendors and end-users want to deal with financial partners who are on "top of their game."

Think BIG and Act With Determination

"Leveraging Relationships"
<u>*Call to Action Questions:*</u>

1) Do you routinely increase the size of a transaction by adding additional equipment?

2) Do your vendors or end-users consider you a primary or secondary source of funding? Are you satisfied with your position or could it be improved?

3) Are you leveraging every relationship?

4) How many relationships do you have that are rock solid and consistently win-win relationships?

5) How many casual relationships do you have that could be improved? What steps need to be taken to fully develop these relationships?

Chapter 3

Ethics

(The most important key to success)

Business Ethics

Businesses are built on integrity, reputation, and value. Business ethics are paramount, and the lack of ethics will quickly result in the demise of any individual or organization. Having strong ethics does not mean individuals will not make mistakes or create challenges for themselves or others.

Your business ethics can be measured best by how you react to difficult situations.

Desperate people do desperate things, and desperation is one of the greatest causes of unethical behavior. It is unfortunate that the unethical behavior of just one person can negatively impact so many. We constantly read sensational articles or news releases of how businesses and business people have taken advantage of society or others who are among the less fortunate. There is an inclination to assume that unethical behavior is the norm in the business community, more specifically, in the leasing and finance industry. I strongly disagree with this unfounded assumption. I know our industry survives because of the trust and honesty that is shared by the majority of individuals who are engaged in the commercial equipment leasing and finance industry. Unfortunately, a few individuals may participate in unethical behavior, bending the rules way too far on a regular basis. However, the industry is quite good at identifying unscrupulous behavior, which results in barring those individuals and organizations.

Commercial equipment leasing and finance professionals are entrusted to be the conduit of information between business clients and ultimate investors. The free flow of information is often measured by speed and ease of the process. In reality, the effectiveness of the flow of information should be primarily measured by the accuracy of information communicated between all parties. Sales and operational professionals manage a two-way speedway of information with many interchangeable parts and players. A challenging process at times, some may feel tempted to move forward by manipulating or eliminating information and necessary verification components.

The manipulation of information is not a gray area; it is unethical and wrong.

Business ethics are defined by what is "right" and what is "wrong." The line is quite thin. Strong, successful veterans in our industry consistently offer their valuable services by conducting themselves well within the boundaries of what is "right" every time. Behaving ethically is tremendously more profitable and rewarding in the long run. The unscrupulous ones will come and go, but the majority who consistency offer strong, honest services will persevere.

I was asked to comment on a particular situation where an originator manipulated information and coached a vendor and lessee to withhold information from a funding source. The originator claimed the process was innocent, performed merely to expedite a large transaction. Nearly a year later, the transaction ran into problems. The client was unable to continue its payments. The funding source quickly discovered that the originator's coaching had jeopardized the funder's collateral position and losses would be incurred. The owner of the origination company (broker) asked what he should do about the funder's potential loss and, equally pressing, what actions should be taken with one of his top sales representatives – the individual who coached the vendor and lessee. The answer was simple: the originator had acted unethically – fraud was committed. The origination company should make the funder whole, terminate the employment of the sales representative,

---

and terminate all relationships with the vendor who had also participated in the fraud. The owner of the origination company was at first reluctant, as the vendor was one of the company's largest sources of business. He claimed the sales rep. and the vendor were his greatest assets. He was mistaken – the sales rep. and the vendor were actually his greatest liabilities.

In a similar situation many years ago, one of the most respected individuals in our industry was devastated by fraudulent behavior committed by one of his employees. The owner of the independent leasing company was the first to discover the fraud. Terminating the employee who was involved in the fraud, the owner immediately notified all of the funders that were affected. It took several years for the independent lessor to make the banks whole. However, the owner worked diligently until the situation was fully resolved. Because of his strong ethical actions, this lessor was never cut off from funding. He grew his business tremendously and built a stronger, more viable business over the coming years. "Right" always prevails.

Business activity is based upon trust and proper actions by all entities. Business reputations take years to build and only minutes to destroy. During challenging times, when profits are depressed, it is even more important to act aboveboard and to be extremely diligent in regard to the actions of others within our organizations, within our business communities and most importantly, in regard to our own individual actions on a daily basis. No transaction or commission (fee income) is worth jeopardizing one's career. Our business is not built with smoke and mirrors – it is dependent upon transparency and accuracy at every level. The entire industry can suffer from the unethical actions of a few.

"Business Ethics"
Call to Action Questions:

1) Have you ever encountered a fraudulent situation?

2) What was your reaction?

3) Do you regularly advocate for the industry?

4) Do you promote your integrity with actions?

5) Would you report fraudulent activities to others in the industry?

Full Disclosure

Strong leasing and finance originators know personal integrity is essential for long-term sustainability. Originators are entrusted with confidential information provided by vendors, lessees, funding sources, credit departments, and other business partners. There is no room for originators who are compelled to manipulate information, to incorrectly represent transactions, or to falsely encourage others to act on misinformation. Savvy originators gather and disseminate information as if their own money were to be invested in every transaction.

Strong credit packages correctly emphasize strengths and correctly point out weaknesses. Originators who gloss over weaknesses or omit weaknesses are acting dishonestly to both themselves and their internal and external partners. Desperation to close a single transaction or generate an insignificant commission is no reason to withhold information that could alter the viability of a transaction.

Integrity is the cornerstone of every business relationship.

You are the eyes and ears of our industry and the industry depends upon your keen senses and gut feelings. There is no need to cut corners or make misrepresentations. You will make significant income and build a strong reputation by conducting yourself ethically.

Present the Facts

"Full Disclosure"
Call to Action Questions:

1) Do you treat all information gathered in the process confidentially?

2) Do you routinely discuss your concerns about particular transactions?

3) Do you ask the tough questions to fully understand transactions?

4) Do you advocate for full-disclosure?

5) Have you ever had a gut feeling that altered your reaction to a transaction?

Reputation is Core

Originators know personal reputations are the key to sustained success. Reputations are built by delivering results, by helping others achieve their goals, and by working to promote best practices within the industry.

An originator encountered the following situation:
A new referral source introduced the originator to a new vendor. Through multiple conversations and meetings, the originator was excited about the vendor's presented opportunity to fund a significant ongoing stream of business. The potential new business would solidify the originator's year, thereby setting him up for an excellent start to the following year. The originator was feeling good that his selling skills had allowed him to win this relationship from a long-term competitor that was falling down on the job. The originator had been waiting for this type of relationship that would rejuvenate his spirit and increase his personal income.

Then he got the call. He discovered the competitor had not lost the relationship, rather the competitor had terminated the relationship because of concerns. One of the partners associated with the vendor had not retired the year before, but had left because of accusations of fraud. Also, multiple accusations surfaced by customers against the vendor such as ongoing interrupted service and broken promises. The vendor tried to assure the originator the situation had been corrected and not to worry, but the originator felt uncomfortable with the facts and explanation. The originator knew he could start the relationship, funding multiple transactions before most of this information became widely known to the public. He knew less savvy originators would jump on the opportunity to make some quick commissions, which meant withholding this crucial information from their credit departments and funding sources.

This seasoned originator knew his reputation was worth more than a few thousand dollars of commissions.

The originator revealed all of the information he had to his credit department and funding source. He informed the vendor and the original referral source that he was unable to proceed with the relationship. In less than 90 days, the originator discovered the vendor was under investigation for fraud and double funding of transactions. The originator had moved on and was busy developing relationships with trusted vendors. He slept well at night.

The Truth & Facts Always Win

"Reputation is Core"
Call to Action Questions:

1) To what length will you go to protect your reputation?

2) If it doesn't feel "right" what are your next steps?

3) How have you shared vital information in the past to protect your internal and external partners?

4) Give examples of how others have shared information with you or your company to protect your interest. What did the sharing of information do to your relationship with this individual or organization?

Chapter 4

Personal Value Proposition (PVP)

A Strong Personal Value Proposition

The commercial equipment leasing and finance industry provides tremendous value to .the U.S. economy. It helps businesses to acquire approximately $900 billion of equipment each year. The greatest value comes from front-line originators who interact directly with their customers. Top originators sell their personal value along with the value of their partners, companies, and industry in order to win more transactions, build better relationships, and provide superior service. They outperform their competition by identifying and aggressively selling their personal value proposition (PVP). The greatest returns are realized when originators move away from commodity offerings and aggressively sell their value over price.

No other competitor has "YOU." It's your knowledge, your persistence, and your attitude that really matter.

Clients buy from you because of who you are. Clients want to buy from the "Real Thing," not an impostor. Therefore, originators need to be able to effectively articulate their uniqueness.

Once you have defined your specific personal value proposition, the sales and marketing process takes on a whole new, powerful dimension. Success is defined by your personal value proposition.

Sell Uniqueness

"A Strong Personal Value Proposition"
Call to Action Questions:

1) What do you personally provide to your clients that are of greatest importance to you?

2) Are your attributes truly unique and why do you consider them important to your relationships?

3) Are the attributes you offer rooted in you, or are they just by-products of your company or the industry as a whole?

4) How do you promote your attributes when you are soliciting new business?

5) Have you asked your clients why they choose you?

Value

If you were a vendor or an end-user, how much would you pay for superior financial services? The best commercial equipment finance and leasing originators sell value over price because they are worth every cent.

A sign in a computer vendor's office read: *"If you pay less for your computers then you are paying way too much. We offer the best value in the market."* The vendor offered value over price. If customers only considered price, then the clients would ultimately get what they paid for – an unsatisfactory buying experience from the vendor's competitors. However, this vendor flaunted high repeat customers and growing corporate clients because of their exceptional value proposition. Corporate clients are willing to pay extra for expertise, superior service, and corporate partners. This message clearly applies to the commercial equipment leasing and finance industry.

The most successful originators promote specific attributes that they are able to offer their clients and are able to justify their value in the market.

Value is sold at every stage of the sales cycle and comes naturally to those professionals who truly believe in themselves. In order to increase production, you must improve your personal value proposition (PVP) and aggressively sell yourself as a meaningful partner in the marketplace. No matter how powerful the product, nothing happens unless you believe in yourself.

Flaunt Value

"Value"
Call to Action Questions:

1) If you were a vendor or end-user would you use the services you provide?

2) Why or why not?

3) Are you worth a higher price?

4) How would you quantify your value?

5) Do you flaunt your PVP or do you regularly fall into pricing wars?

Creating Opportunities

Leasing and finance originators with a strong personal value proposition (PVP) are optimistic. Seeing an opportunity in every new challenge, they are creative enough to provide solutions when their competitors fall short with a boiler-plate mentality.

Pessimistic conclusions are excuses for lack of desire to succeed: *no one is buying right now, the pricing is too high, the credit department never approves any transactions, or all of my customers are paying cash.* All of these statements are pessimistic statements that are simply not true. No matter what the economic climate, there are always deals to be funded.

The opportunistic originator is a realist and faces challenges head on.

Challenge: Competition is tougher today than in the past.

Solution: *Clients are asking more questions and verifying each transaction more carefully; however, I am adding value to the process because of my understanding of my products and because of my consultative selling approach. As a leasing/finance advisor, I am winning more transactions by creating value for my vendors and end-users and allowing them to be more successful.*

Successful originators are confident in their ability to deliver "real value" every day and never underestimate their ability to outperform their competition. They act as entrepreneurs by offering superior service at a fair price.

Success is a Choice

"Creating Opportunities"
Call to Action Questions:

1) Do you face challenges with optimistic solutions?

2) Do you create new opportunities for yourself?

3) Does your personal value proposition attract new opportunities?

4) Do you facilitate a process of bringing stakeholders together?

5) Do you regularly flaunt your optimism?

Creating a PVP

Every originator has value to offer her clients – the secret is the ability to identify and articulate a strong personal value proposition (PVP).

The process of developing a powerful PVP is personal. Once accomplished, the sales and marketing process becomes more meaningful and effective.

There are many different questions you should consider when developing your personal value proposition. Below are a few questions that you should ask:

- What experiences do you specifically bring to a transaction/relationship?
- What verifiable expertise do you have?
- What level of knowledge do you have in regard to the products and services you specifically offer?
- What level of knowledge do you have in regard to the products and services that are available in the market?
- What attributes are you looking for in a stakeholder?
- What do you offer that no one else in the market can offer?
- How are you going to strengthen your uniqueness?
- What are your personal weaknesses? How will you mitigate these challenges?
- What is your personal passion? How do you express it best?

One of the best means of developing a PVP is to ask top clients what value they perceive you bring to the process.

Write It Down

"Creating a PVP"
<u>*Call to Action Questions:*</u>

1) Write down five attributes you bring to the process.

2) Has your personal value proposition evolved over time?

3) Why are these attributes powerful, unique, and important to you and your clients?

4) How can you better articulate these attributes?

5) Repeat steps one through four and continue the process until you are satisfied with your PVP.

Solutions

Personal value propositions (PVP) are solution based and consider the needs of vendors and end-users. Successful originators are an integral part of the selling cycle and offer specific value to the process. The most successful originators embrace:

- Listening, learning, and acting.
- Change.
- Stepping outside of a comfort zone to create opportunity.
- Starting new marketing initiatives.
- Leveraging past experiences to create new opportunities.
- Prospecting with purpose.
- 100% focus on success and growth.
- New challenges.

Delivering solutions requires you to continuously prospect, learn, and inject yourself into an ever-changing market.

Personal value propositions have the flexibility to conform to many different challenges and offer "real" solutions for vendors and end-users. The most successful originators are capable of anticipating future needs and challenges. They embrace change in the market by providing meaningful, forward-thinking solutions for their vendors and end-users.

PVP's are Solution Based

"Solutions"
<u>*Call to Action Questions:*</u>

1) Can you quantify your expertise?

2) What specific solutions do you provide to your vendors and/or end-users?

3) Do you listen, learn, and act?

4) Do you embrace change and new opportunities?

5) Are you part of the solution for your clients?

6) Provide a specific example of how you have conquered a challenge for your clients.

Chapter 5

Soliciting Vendors
&
End-users

Vendor or End-user

Should commercial equipment leasing and finance originators focus on either the vendor or end-user channel? Perhaps both?

One channel is not necessarily better than another channel; they are just different. The most successful originators have an appreciation for both channels, and many top producers can be equally successful calling on both vendors and end-users. A complete understanding of the industry includes knowing how the products and services of the commercial equipment leasing and finance industry benefit both vendors and end-users, how the different parties interact, and, most importantly, how a strong originator plays an integral role in providing superior services that satisfy the needs of all stakeholders.

The best means of building a strong end-user relationship is through a vendor introduction. The best means of building a strong vendor relationship is through an end-user introduction.

You should neither abandon your current channel nor shift your current solicitation focus. The best vendor-driven originators leverage their relationships and build meaningful, ongoing relationships with many of the strongest end-users that were introduced to them through their vendor channels. End-user-driven originators have direct interactions with valuable vendors that were introduced to them through end-user relationships. As a strong originator, you must leverage every relationship to build a wider network of stakeholders.

Expand Opportunities

"Vendor or End-User"
Call to Action Questions:

1) Are you vendor or end-user focused?

2) Do you leverage your relationships to find new stakeholders on a regular basis?

3) Are you blinded by your primary focus and leaving low hanging opportunities unsolicited?

4) Give an example of a new vendor opportunity developed through an end-user; or an end-user that was further developed after referred to by a vendor.

Penetration

The goal of leasing and finance originators is to expand the universe of individuals who know about their services.

Vendors: Successful originators make it a point when calling vendors to verify all of the names of current sales representatives within each vendor. They reach out and touch each sales rep. – not just the rep. who provided the last transaction. Top originators ask their current contacts to refer others within the company; an internal referral is easy and will quickly increase vendor penetration. Strong originators know the sales manager, the owner, the sales coordinator, the new sales representatives, the top producer, the trainee, and/or even the CFO. Each vendor within your CRM system should have multiple contacts in order to maximize your effectiveness and personal income.

End-users: Successful originators make it a point when calling end-users to continuously add new contacts. Working the ladder of authority within each end-user will assist in developing a thorough understanding of their needs, thus better serving the client. Your relationships will become stronger and your personal income will increase with each new contact.

A database with single contacts lacks penetration and creates missed opportunities.

When you strive for better penetration with every call and meeting, you will build quality relationships.

Broaden Influence Daily

"Penetration"
Call to Action Questions:

1) Do you rank your contacts and companies within your CRM system? How effective is your ranking system?

2) Do you periodically update your contact lists to make sure they are always current?

3) How many new contacts have you added to your CRM in the last week/month/quarter?

4) Could you add additional contacts in your top relationships?

5) What is holding you back?

Knowing the Vendor

Originators are often asked to provide a vendor profile with credit packages and many originators cringe at the request. Strong sales professionals embrace vendor profiles.

In order to properly solicit business and to effectively provide superior vendor services, you must know your vendors.

Your profile should include, but not be limited to:

- The type of equipment sold.
- The financial strength of the vendor.
- The ownership of the vendor operation.
- The territory the vendor serves.
- The experience of the sales team.
- The challenges the vendor faces.
- The percentage of revenues that are funded through outside financing sources.
- Past leasing/finance partners.
- The current status of your relationship with the vendor.

Strong vendor profiles confirm your professionalism in knowing your business partners. As a strong originator, you may want to include the credit department in the profiling process and provide vendor information prior to the first credit submission.

Build Strong Profiles

"Knowing the Vendor"
Call to Action Questions:

1) Do you maintain up-to-date vendor profiles?

2) How well do you know your top ten vendors on a scale of 1- 5?

3) What are the three main challenges of your primary vendors?

4) Do you share vendor information with others in your organization?

5) How can vendor profiles help your organization grow and improve your personal income?

6) Do you have a list of questions that you routinely use to build meaningful vendor profiles?

Knowing the End-user

The strongest commercial equipment leasing and finance originators think long term when building relationships with their end-users. They build comprehensive profiles on their customers and keep track of their end-user's progress.

Relationships are built with meaningful information.

By fully understanding an end-user's wants, needs, and credit worthiness, you can provide more meaningful solutions and stronger services. It is not difficult for average originators to conduct investigations and discover most general attributes related to any end-users (Google, websites, public information). However, you will build better relationships with decision makers, understand your end-users, and win more transactions through direct communications.

The strongest originators <u>never</u> shy away from asking the tough questions. With extensive profiles, you can anticipate buying patterns, turn smaller requests into multiple schedules, and leverage every relationship. By knowing your customers, you will work smarter, maximize your effectiveness in the market, and outsell your competition.

Explore Farther

"Knowing the End-user"
Call to Action Questions:

1) Do you maintain up-to-date end-user profiles?

2) Is your information gathered through public sources, through personal contacts (discussions) or both?

3) How well do you know your top ten end-users on a scale of 1- 5?

4) How often do you build credit files on potential customers without being requested by your credit department?

5) Are your profiles readily shared with others in your organization?

Consistent Communication

Strong commercial equipment leasing and finance originators possess the ability to engage in sincere conversations with their vendors and end-users. Selling techniques always include the ability to listen and present compelling benefits regarding products and services. In surveys, both end-users and vendors list strong communication as one of the most important qualities they expect from their financial partners. Business partners are willing and able to converse on multiple levels; relationships are built by sharing information, concerns, suggestions, and ideas. Many relationships can be strengthened by open conversations, especially when details are complex or confusing to the vendor or end-user.

Vendors and end-users want to align themselves with smart business partners who are able to communicate their value and capabilities.

Communication is essential. You should never assume your partners are up-to-date. You must constantly reach out and confirm your relationships. Sincere conversations allow clients to understand your "true" expertise and ability to service their needs. The strongest originators are great communicators.

Engage with Your Clients

> ### *"Consistent Communication"*
> ### <u>*Call to Action Questions:*</u>
>
> 1) Do your clients demand an open line
>   of communication?
>
> 2) Do you maintain strong communication
>   with your top relationships?
>
> 3) Do you maintain strong communication
>   with your prospects?
>
> 4) Do you quickly disseminate both positive
>   and negative outcomes to your
>   vendors/end-users?
>
> 5) Do you ask your clients the best means of
>   staying in touch?

Suggestive Selling

Suggestive selling is all about defining a challenge and then suggesting viable solutions. The below examples are not meant to be a script, but a conceptual dialogue to encourage originators to have a more meaningful conversation with their prospects.

Vendor Solution: "Delayed purchases or reduced purchases are generally caused by cash flow concerns. I work closely with my top vendors to provide real cash flow solutions for their clients and move their customers closer to a sale more quickly. *(Provide a specific example of how you have helped a vendor in the recent past.)* I would like to work with you in the same capacity and help you to move your prospects from uncertainty to a satisfied customer."

End-User Solution: "I know capital is always an issue when making purchases. Therefore, I work closely with my clients to provide them the "right" financial solutions to allow their businesses to be more efficient and for them to buy the equipment they need to grow and outperform their competition. My products and services have helped others in your industry to move forward and to prosper in today's economy. *(Provide an actual example).* I would be delighted to offer these same products to your company."

Top producing originators flex their capabilities and project confidence as they help businesses (vendors and end-users) grow and prosper.

The more specifics you can provide in your solutions – the more powerful your suggestions become.

Create Your Own Opportunities

"Suggestive Selling"
Call to Action Questions:

1) Do you react to challenges with a suggestive solution?

2) Do you perceive yourself as an advisor or a sales person?

3) Are you pro-active in your sales approach? Or reactive?

4) Do you provide examples of how you have helped other vendors or end-users in the past?

5) Give an example of how a suggestive approach has helped you win a relationship or transaction in the past.

Chapter 6

Credit & Pricing

The Total Transaction

"I am the sales guy not the credit manager. Why do I need to know how to analyze a credit package?"

The best credit professionals understand the sales process and top performing sales professionals have a great working knowledge of the credit process.

Strong originators aren't frustrated by credit decisions because they take the time and effort to understand the total transaction. Successful originators ask the tough questions, review financial statements (if necessary), and properly package their transactions before submitting them to the credit department. Top producers work closely with their credit departments in order to solicit, process, and fund high quality transactions that meet the criteria of their companies or funding partners.

To be an accomplished originator you need to have meaningful conversations with your credit departments and be equally at ease speaking to corporate controllers and chief financial officers. You should fully understand why transactions are approved and why they may be declined. Your credit expertise will help to expedite the credit process, address potential credit challenges, and save everyone time and energy. Your monthly and annual results will be quickly enhanced when you focus on transactions that can be funded – and when you have a complete understanding of, and are fully engaged in, the credit process.

Strong Credit Decisions Start with the Originator

"The Total Transaction"
Call to Action Questions:

1) Are you well aware of the credit criteria of your company (or funding sources)?

2) When was the last time you discussed credit policy with a credit manager?

3) Are you comfortable speaking with a controller, accountant, or owner about your client's financial position?

4) Do you have the skills to approve a transaction and the discipline to reject a transaction?

5) If it were your money, would you invest in your own transactions? Why? Or why not?

The Equipment Matters

The commercial equipment leasing and finance industry provides funds for the acquisition of "ESSENTIAL" equipment. The determination of whether or not a transaction includes essential equipment is dependent upon the users as much as the equipment itself.

Originators need to explore the equipment and the purpose of the acquisition.

Too often, originators make over-reaching assumptions regarding the equipment. Therefore, it is important to remind originators of the basic questions that should always be addressed:

- Why is the client acquiring the equipment?
- Is the equipment income producing?
- Is the equipment replacement equipment or additional equipment?
- Will the equipment improve efficiencies and reduce cost?
- Is the equipment new or used?
- Is the equipment tier one or tier two equipment? (A Cadillac may be tier one and a Chevy tier three)
- Why is this acquisition and equipment essential to this client?
- Does this acquisition make sense?

By recognizing the importance of the equipment and asking all of the pertinent questions regarding specific equipment, you will increase your value to your vendors, end-users, and credit departments.

Be an Equipment Expert

"The Equipment Matters"
<u>*Call to Action Questions:*</u>

1) Do you have strong equipment knowledge?

2) Do you ask how the equipment will be used and how it will impact the client's business?

3) Give an example of non-essential equipment.

4) Give examples of tier one and tier three equipment. Why does this matter?

5) How can the same piece of equipment be essential for customer A, but non-essential for customer B?

6) What are the eventual challenges when funding non-essential equipment?

Risk and Reward

The commercial equipment leasing and finance industry is a risk/reward business and originators should treat it as such. Not every transaction deserves the lowest yield. It is the originator's responsibility to analyze a particular transaction and determine, based upon the financial strength and potential risk of an individual customer, how a transaction should be priced.

In order to survive in the leasing and finance market, a successful originator must be able to review financial statements, tax returns, industry trends, and the overall strengths and weaknesses of a transaction. How can an originator offer the correct products, structure, or pricing unless he understands the risk of the transaction?

The market does not allow an originator to be fruitful if he only offers "one size fits all" solutions.

The greatest disparity between success and mediocrity in our industry is caused by a lack of credit understanding, and risk versus reward awareness.

The best means of maximizing your income potential is to have a complete understanding of the market forces. A complete understanding will allow you to spend more time on transactions which match your funding capabilities and prevent you from leaving valuable profits on the table. By understanding all of the market forces you will also reduce your frustrations, allowing you to focus on SUCCESS.

Know the Market

"Risk and Reward"
Call to Action Questions:

1) Do you consider risk when pricing your transactions?

2) Do you and your company get paid for the risk it assumes?

3) Do you make every effort to fully understand your transactions before they are priced? Before they are submitted to credit?

4) Does the credit process frustrate you? How well do you understand the credit criteria you are selling?

5) Do you solicit transactions that are winnable and within your funding capabilities?

Financial Analysis

The strongest leasing and finance originators are well versed in financial analysis. The day will arrive for every originator when it is necessary to have basic financial analysis knowledge, even if an originator dominantly participates in the application only arena. An originator can fully understand a client when he analyzes the financial condition of the operation. Relationships are built upon demonstrating a sincere interest in what creates success for a potential customer. Financial statements reflect how a potential customer is able to create success on a regular basis. To advise a client on how commercial leasing and finance products will best meet a company's needs, an originator must understand how a potential client has financed its past growth.

Successful originators invest in themselves.

Originators are confident in both their selling skills and their ability to analyze the financial condition of their clients. They take the time to review basic financial ratios (i.e. debt to equity, liquidity, current ratio, debt coverage, etc.), and they actually read the financial notes that accompany the financial statement.

To be a successful originator, take the time and energy to develop analytical skills. Spend time engaging with your credit departments. Embrace the opportunity to discuss financial conditions with your clients. Build relationships based upon your own knowledge and advisory skills regarding the financial strength of your clients. This way, you will save the time and energy of your entire team by pre-qualifying your clients on a regular basis.

The Numbers are Worth Reading

"Financial Analysis"
Call to Action Questions:

1) Can you package a full disclosure credit transaction?

2) What is an acceptable leverage position for the industries you solicit?

3) What is an acceptable net profit margin for the industries you solicit?

4) What is the difference between a tangible and non-tangible equity position?

5) What can be revealed in the financial notes of a company?

6) Why can tax returns and financial statements have different financial results?

Competitively Priced

Originators and organizations need to properly price their products in order to be competitive in the market and drive new business volume. Properly priced does not mean that you have offered your products at the lowest possible price in the market. It means that you offer a fair price for exceptional value. The most successful originators sell value over price. Originators have the responsibility to find transactions that properly match their capabilities and yield requirements.

If price were the only determining factor in creating new business, then there would be no need to have a sales force.

Originators who argue for below market pricing to drive business are, in essence, communicating their lack of ability to add value to every transaction.

Strong originators know they may not win every transaction; however, they don't immediately default to reduced pricing when negotiations get tough. They lead with value and end with value. Top producers offer competitive pricing and are willing to earn a premium for their services. There is no shame in losing a transaction when an originator offers his best. Shame comes from never knowing a transaction existed. Shame comes from unnecessarily cutting one's profits.

The commercial equipment leasing and finance industry is highly competitive. You should always sell value over price in order to maintain a sustainable business model for all economies. The strongest clients will appreciate your professionalism and be willing to pay a fair price for exceptional service.

Get Paid for Your Value

Call to Action

"Competitively Priced"
Call to Action Questions:

1) Are you the lowest priced provider of your services?

2) How do you promote your value over a competitor's lower price?

3) How much extra are you worth in the market?

4) Who is your biggest competitor and why?

5) Give an example of a transaction won when you were clearly higher in price.

Structures

Leasing and finance originators must have a complete understanding of how transactions are priced and structured in the market. Every structure includes five key elements:

- Term of the transaction
- Reward – desired yield
- Risk – the client's credit worthiness
- Up-front monies
- End of term options

The alteration of either one or any combination of the above elements changes the entire structure and pricing of any transaction.

Strong originators ask pertinent questions to determine what structures their clients prefer, what alternative structures their clients may consider, and what they are competing against in the market.

Strong originators know the impact difference between advance payments compared to down payments or security deposits. They know the impact of a fair market value lease over a $1.00 buyout or guaranteed purchase option (PUT). They know the competitive structures that they are competing against and can sell the benefits of their structures and pricing with confidence.

You should always dissect your competitors' proposals, understand their structures, and know how your programs are positioned in the market. Pricing and structure knowledge is imperative for success.

Dissect the Structural Details

"Structures"
Call to Action Questions:

1) Are you proficient in dissecting competitors' proposals?

2) What happens to the monthly payments when a fair market value assumption is increased? Decreased?

3) How can credit risk be mitigated through a change in the structure?

4) What upfront money would decrease the monthly payments more: two advance payments or a security deposit equal to two payments?

5) What are the criteria for a tax lease?

6) What are the criteria for an FASB 13 operating lease?

7) How do deferred payments impact the monthly payments?

Documentation

Commercial equipment leasing and finance agreements are legal contracts and should be treated as such. Originators need to understand their processes, pricing, structures, competition, credit requirements, and clients. But, they also need to understand their documentation because these legal documents are the foundation of the process. I am often reminded of how many originators have little or no knowledge about the content and meaning behind the legal documentation that they routinely ask their customers to sign.

All originators should read and understand their documents.

Legal documents protect the originator and his company. Every sentence and paragraph has a purpose. Understanding leasing and finance documentation confirms the originator's acknowledgement that the transaction does not end when the transaction is funded and the sales commission is received. In fact, the transaction is "JUST BEGINNING." The documentation clarifies the client's responsibility to properly perform and repay its obligations; it outlines the product that the originator is truly selling.

As a successful originator, you must have a complete understanding of your documentation, be prepared to discuss the contents, and defend each provision.

Read - Understand - Sell

"Documentation"
<u>*Call to Action Questions:*</u>

1) Have you read your lease documents lately?

2) If you were called upon to defend your documentation in court would you be comfortable taking the stand?

3) Do you regularly explain different documentation provisions to your clients?

4) Pursuant to your documents:
   - When are late charges assessed?
   - What insurance responsibilities does the lessee have?
   - What are the return, renewal or purchase options available under the agreement?
   - What is a Master Lease agreement?
   - What are the responsibilities of the client if the equipment does not perform properly?

Chapter 7

Time Management

Distractions

Time management is the key to success. Originators are at their best when they are busy with productive activities. However, originators are often distracted with non-productive activities.

Strong originators know time is money. Lost time can never be regained. Therefore, successful originators are focused on outcomes, building the "right" relationships, asking the hard qualifying questions early in the process, and quickly eliminating distractions that limit their ability to maximize personal incomes.

No matter how strong a marketing plan, it is the execution of the plan that determines success.

Your execution of a marketing plan or strategy is based upon your ability to stay focused on those activities that move you forward. Busy work is counterproductive and hinders "real" results. Take inventory of your time and activities to determine when you are most productive and when you easily are distracted. Money is made when you are more efficient and concentrate on those activities that align with your personal goals, objectives, and strategies.

Focus on Outcomes

"Distractions"
<u>*Call to Action Questions:*</u>

1) How much time is being spent interacting with end-users, vendors and business partners that can truly advance your ability to increase sales and personal incomes?

2) How can you work more efficiently?

3) What can be done to work smarter?

4) Is time being wasted on clients that have limited potential?

5) Have you taken inventory of how you spend a typical day? Where your efforts could be improved? And what lost opportunities you are allowing to occur?

A Fluid Database

Do you have a strong database? Is your database a thriving source of new business? Many leasing and finance originators find comfort in having a large database of potential vendors and end-users. However, upon closer examination, their databases are nearly stagnant, comprised of the same contacts and companies that were present twelve months ago or even six years ago. An active database should be constantly changing. The economy changes, most originators' capabilities change, and the needs of potential clients change. Therefore, successful originators are constantly updating their databases. Expansion and contraction of a database reflects an originator's true effort to penetrate a market and flush out those clients that are best served by her capabilities. Strong database management is essential for an originator to maximize her income potential.

The quality of an active database is more important than its size; quality should be defined by the alignment of the database with the funding capabilities of the originator.

You should be willing to have a smaller, yet stronger database. Your time should be spent qualifying prospects and calling on the best potential clients, rather than continuing to call on non-prospects who are easy to contact, yet have little, if any, potential to become a viable customer.

Quality Always Trumps Quantity

"A Fluid Database"
<u>*Call to Action Questions:*</u>

1) Is your database up-to-date?

2) Does your database expand and contract regularly? How many contacts do you currently have? How many contacts did you have six months ago? One year ago? Is your database fluid?

3) On average, how many contacts do you have for each end-user or vendor you call upon? Is this enough? Does your CRM reflect all of your contacts?

4) If you were out of the office and a co-worker was asked to help one of your clients, would your CRM notes clearly reflect your relationship?

Setting Expectations

The best means of saving time and energy is to properly set expectations for all involved in a transaction. Most commercial equipment leasing and finance originators are impatient. Sometimes, in the pursuit of driving new business and moving transactions forward, originators waste time by needlessly backing themselves into corners that are hard to escape.

Top producers in the industry know the power of under promising and over delivering on their services.

Strong originators set expectations upfront and work diligently to make sure every expectation is met on time, every time.

Customers would prefer a meaningful answer in two days, rather than a wrong answer or half answer in two hours. Customers would prefer hearing: "I don't know, but I will find out and get back to you," rather than "I'm sorry, but I gave you the wrong information this morning."

You should have meaningful conversations with your end-users and vendors to navigate the prospect through the process. It is through conversations that originators build meaningful, long lasting relationships. During these conversations, it is important to manage expectations and to create an environment whereby you can easily over deliver on every promise.

Under Promise and Over Deliver

"Setting Expectations"
Call to Action Questions:

1) Do you consistently meet your client's expectations?

2) Are you willing to say: "I don't know, but I will find out."?

3) What do you do when you find yourself backed into a corner? How does this happen?

4) Do you have meaningful conversations with your customers?

5) Do you fully explain the process upfront?

Celebrate

Success for equipment leasing and finance originators is a process. One strong month is not a trend. A few deals from a vendor do not necessarily indicate a long-term relationship. One large transaction, allowing an originator to make her budget for the quarter, doesn't necessarily indicate excellence. However, all are steps toward success and should be celebrated.

Celebrations encourage optimism.

Celebrations confirm positive perspectives that can, and should, be transferred to customers, vendors, partners and internal stakeholders. Celebrations along the path to success remind us of our progress and create an atmosphere of joy, self-confidence, and professionalism. The opportunities in the market grow on a daily basis for originators who are focused and willing to maximize their time and energy. Originators need to be enthusiastically attacking the market with a "can do" attitude, all the while making additional efforts to prospect and win stronger clients. It takes persistence to break down barriers and reach powerful decision makers who are able to award stronger, more viable transactions.

Emphasizing your accomplishments will allow you to combine small steps into larger, more meaningful successes. You need to celebrate the process of building a path toward success. You will continue to learn, build additional relationships, provide better service, and celebrate larger success.

Celebrate Real Achievements

"Celebrate"
<u>*Call to Action Questions:*</u>

1) Do you celebrate your successes?

2) What does a celebration look like?

3) Do you create stretch goals and then "step it up" to accomplish them?

4) When was your last celebration as an individual? As a team?

5) List three to five accomplishments that you have made in the last week. In the last six months.

Deadlines

Successful equipment leasing and finance professionals know the power of deadlines. People are motivated to act when confronted by a deadline. Taxes are filed by April 15th. Vendors push to deliver equipment by month end. Work is completed before the boss leaves for vacation. One of the key responsibilities of a strong originator is to orchestrate the timing of a transaction. Every day's activities are critical to meeting monthly and annual goals. The business environment is made up of many procrastinators who constantly delay actions, which, at times, impedes the ability of originators to meet their goals.

The strongest originators announce their timelines to all participants.

- I need to have the documents back by Friday, in order to finalize the transaction by the end of the month.
- My goal is to have a completed application and your request submitted to the credit department by tomorrow afternoon.
- I will contact your accountant by 2:00 this afternoon so a final decision can be rendered before the end of the day.
- I need a vendor invoice as soon as possible to have the money wired this afternoon.

By creating deadlines, you will create a sense of urgency. Urgency creates opportunities for both you and your company. As a successful professional you can use deadlines to motivate others to act, reach corporate and individual goals, and produce real results.

Meeting Deadlines is Essential

"Deadlines"
Call to Action Questions:

1) Do you set deadlines and are you able to meet them regularly?

2) Are you instrumental in creating a sense of urgency for others?

3) Do you work well under pressure?

4) Do you control the timing of your transactions? Why? Or why not?

5) Who sets the most deadlines? You? Your boss? Your vendors? Your end-users? (Whoever sets the timing controls the transaction.)

Double/Triple/Quadruple Production

What must be true for successful commercial equipment leasing and finance originators to double, triple or quadruple their current production?

Many originators cannot conceive how they could possibly do more business without working eighteen hours a day, six days a week.

Top producers work smarter and harder than the average originators; they spend their time on activities that produce the greatest results.

Top producers are focused. They measure their activities to determine which tasks can be improved upon and which simply need to be eliminated.

Originators must let the process work efficiently and have faith in their stakeholders (vendors, funders, credit departments and end-users) to actively participate in the process. Leveraging your team and partners is the key to increased production. However, you do not want to lose touch with the process. A fine line exists between over involvement and neglect. A transaction can easily fall through the cracks if neglected.

Working smarter does not mean working less; it requires you to use your valuable time more wisely. You can exponentially increase (double, triple, quadruple) your results by taking control of activities, orchestrating the process, and pursuing those opportunities that deliver the greatest results.

Make Every Day Count

Double/Triple/Quadruple Production"
Call to Action Questions:

1) Could you double your production in the next six months? What must be true for such an increase to occur?

2) What activities would need to be eliminated to increase your production?

3) Do you measure your time and productivity?

4) What counterproductive activities have you participated in over the last week?

5) What steps do you need to take to be a more effective originator?

Marketing Automation

Significant progress has been made in marketing automation. Leasing and finance originators who effectively use strong *contact relationship management* (CRM) systems significantly increase their personal production numbers.

Strong, industry specific CRM systems allow individual originators to leverage every contact, systematically increasing their ability to touch more prospects and better serve the needs of their clients.

A well-performing CRM system allows marketing teams to increase their production numbers by as much as 20%. Strong systems allow originators to share information effectively with vendors, end-users, credit, and funding departments. They are able to complete marketing campaigns easily, and most importantly, originators are able to save valuable time. Additionally, industry specific CRM systems help an organization manage workflow, analyze trends, and improve risk management – efficiencies that improve company performance and secure their market position.

Marketing automation is an essential tool to enable you to be a top producer. As a successful originator, you should be expanding the use of automation, constantly pushing your systems to greater limits, and seeking new means to leverage your systems to gain the greatest outcomes.

Leverage Your Marketing Efforts

"Marketing Automation"
__*Call to Action Questions:*__

1) Do you use a strong CRM effectively?

2) How does your CRM allow you to better serve the needs of your clients?

3) Do you use your CRM as your primary depository of information? Why or why not?

4) Explain how your CRM saves you time and helps you to increase business.

5) Do you push your CRM to its limits?

Striking a Balance

How an originator spends his time makes the difference between mediocrity and success. Most individuals log in forty to fifty hours a week dedicated to their profession. The secret is to strike a balance between servicing existing clients and prospecting for new vendors and end-users; strike a balance between preparing for a sales call and actually delivering a great presentation; strike a balance between marketing and operational activities.

Successful leasing and finance originators are exemplary time managers.

A strong originator, with a long running and once highly profitable program faced a common dilemma. The program and equipment type had become highly commoditized – margins had consistently been compressed over the last few years. The originator was easily spending 40% or greater of his time servicing his relationships, but the program accounted for less than 15% of his income, with no improving results. In contrast, one of his newer initiatives was producing greater results, accounting for nearly 30% of his bottom line production with an allocation of only about 20% of his time. The pure numbers indicated an easy decision to re-allocate his time from less productive opportunities to more productive activities. But, the less productive programs were well within the originator's comfort zone.

To be successful, you need to strike a balance, know what efforts are forward thinking and future trending. You must always compare comfort zones with opportunities and invest your efforts based upon facts rather than emotions.

Increase Productivity

"Striking a Balance"
Call to Action Questions:

1) Do you know which of your relationships are most profitable?

2) Do you allocate your time and resources based upon profitability potential?

3) Do you get emotionally attached to less productive relationships?

4) Describe your comfort zone. Is it a profitable zone? How can it be expanded? Or reduced?

5) How do you motivate yourself to move outside of your comfort zone?

Chapter 8

Self-Development

Invest in Yourself

Originators in the commercial equipment leasing and finance industry control their own destiny. Success is directly related to personal effort. Having a passion for the industry, originators enjoy the process of offering superior financial services to their vendors and end-users. Leasing and finance originators make daily choices in regard to how they invest their time, effort, money, and talents. No one else knows their abilities better than they. Originators know when they are in a productive zone as they create and maximize real worth for their clients.

Strong originators look inward, adjusting to the market when necessary. Originators invest in themselves and improve their offerings in the market by updating their knowledge and expertise. *The work of a leasing and finance originator is not a 9 to 5 job.* Creative minds are constantly thinking of new ways to market, reach additional clients, and provide better services. A successful originator does not see his career as a means to an end, but as an exciting, ongoing journey that is constantly evolving as new opportunities appear.

Before you can ask others to invest in your services, you must be willing to aggressively invest in yourself.

The industry provides you with unlimited opportunities and will reward you for persistence, creativity, and professionalism.

The Market Will Reward Those Who are Vested

"Invest in Yourself"
Call to Action Questions:

1) Describe a specific investment you are making in yourself.

2) Do others invest in you because they know you are vested in the industry?

3) Do you flaunt your personal investment in the industry and yourself?

4) How can additional investments help you to advance your career?

5) Is commercial equipment leasing/finance a job or a vocation to you?

6) Describe a transition that you experienced in the past and how you looked inwardly to improve your personal skills.

Personal Advisory Team

Many successful corporations have an advisory board to provide insightful discussions and advice concerning new ideas. Originators should also have a team of advisors. The team should be comprised of individuals with different experiences in order to provide the originator with diverse resources and perspectives. The advisory team should include valued mentors – individuals who are respected, but don't necessarily always agree with each other or the originator.

Strong originators have developed many relationships with internal and external individuals who are excellent sounding boards to discuss new opportunities and challenges.

A true advisory team is a formal and steadfast group with whom the originator routinely meets.

This team need not be large, in fact, the meeting may or may not be conducted as a group; however, it is important for the originator to share all vital information with the entire team, thus soliciting suggestions from each member.

Your career development will be expedited when opportunities and challenges are vetted through an advisory team that is not emotionally connected to every situation. You will need to be open to competing ideas and constructive criticism in order to formulate new strategies. A strong advisory board can confirm commitment and assign purpose to your long-term objectives.

Build a Strong Team

"Personal Advisory Team"
Call to Action Questions:

1) Do you have a personal advisory board or mentors?

2) Who is your best mentor and why?

3) Who should be added to your advisory board?

4) How often do you meet or speak to your personal board?

5) Do you accept criticism well?

6) How has constructive criticism helped you to improve in the past?

Dynamic Leaders

Originators are often rightfully recognized for large achievements: producing high monthly sales, landing large accounts, developing new niches, etc. Sustainable, long-term success is achieved through a process. The process includes daily commitment, risk-taking, learning, and exploring new opportunities. The strongest originators are never satisfied with the status quo. They know that standing still means falling behind. The strongest originators are innovative leaders.

Assuming the role as a dynamic leader in the industry requires originators to engage with the industry, learn from their competition, and listen to their vendors and end-users.

Leaders have a realistic "can-do" attitude. The strongest originators are proactive, based upon an ongoing gathering of intelligence. Dynamic leaders are solution providers, rather than order takers, advisors rather than salespeople, and investigators rather than individuals who base actions on false assumptions. Originators explore how others have accomplished success. Instead of emulating others, originators learn from their predecessors and contemporaries, thus creating original marketing strategies that lead to success.

To be your best you need to attack the market from a leader's perspective, add value to the process, and offer your personal experiences. Success is a continuous learning experience, filled with creativity and leadership.

Learn, Grow, Succeed

"Dynamic Leaders"
<u>*Call to Action Questions:*</u>

1) Do you consider yourself a dynamic leader in the company? Industry?

2) What have you learned from other leaders?

3) Do you innovate and offer new solutions?

4) How do you flaunt your passion for success?

5) How would you describe your current learning process? What is on the front burner? What is on the back burner and why?

The Tenacious Originator

Strong leasing and finance originators stick to their plans and continue to work hard even when the going gets tough. The best means of increasing production numbers is to hold firm to the process and engage with the "right" end-users and vendors. Originators who have the tenacity to move relationships forward while continuing to seek out new prospects will always come out ahead of the pack.

Originators willing to go the extra mile from the beginning of the process, seeking the best path rather than the easiest path, are the originators who are outperforming their peers. Providing the best service in the commercial equipment leasing and finance industry is not about cutting corners, but about properly navigating the process with conviction and expertise. Originators provide value when they are willing to ask the tough questions, anticipate challenges, and provide concise solutions upfront. Tenacious originators do not wander from plan A to plan B. They have purpose behind every call as they execute their plan.

Your tenacity will set you apart from the competition.

Not only will you gain respect, but also deliver better results when you stick to a comprehensive marketing plan that aligns with who you are and what you are trying to accomplish.

Commit to Your Success

"The Tenacious Originator"
Call to Action Questions:

1) Do you have a well thought out marketing plan and strategy?

2) Do you work your plan on a daily basis?

3) Do you seek the right path or the easiest path?

4) Can you articulate your plan?

5) Do you consider yourself a tenacious professional? Why or why not?

Fun

Leasing and finance originators know that the business can be challenging at times. However, it can all be worth the effort when the primary description of the day is "FUN."

- In what other industry can a professional engage with multiple businesses and help entrepreneurs, small businesses, and Fortune 500 companies grow and prosper?
- In what other industry can a professional have access to confidential financial information that accurately reflects how small, medium, and large businesses are adjusting in order to thrive in the world's largest economy?
- In what other industry can a professional build business relationships with multiple equipment vendors that will leverage her efforts and allow for real industry penetration?
- In what other industry can a professional be rewarded so greatly for her own efforts to offer innovative financial solutions based upon a free market?

Successful originators enjoy the process while embracing the growing opportunities that continue to develop in the market.

As financial advisors, you are providing indispensable solutions. Enjoy digging deeply into every relationship in order to fully understand your lessees, vendors, and transactions.

Embrace Your Position

"Fun"
<u>*Call to Action Questions:*</u>

1) Are you having fun on a daily basis?

2) Do you embrace the process and gain personal satisfaction by helping businesses grow?

3) Do you understand the power of your position? And how you help others succeed?

4) Do you offer "real" solutions to your clients in a positive manner?

5) Describe an example of how you, or the industry, affect the entire economy.

Claim Responsibility

Originators in the commercial equipment leasing and finance industry have an entrepreneurial spirit. They obtain job security by taking responsibility for their results. In a highly competitive environment, the strongest originators are not shy about trying new tactics to build their businesses, develop new relationships, and create new business channels. Success often requires professionals to confidently take calculated risks. Part of success is the ability to accept failures, to learn from mistakes, and to persevere to a higher level.

The strongest equipment leasing and finance originators are willing to step out onto the stage and put themselves into the spotlight.

It's easy to stay in a comfort zone, continue calling on the same safe customer and remain relatively safe within the status-quo arena with minimal growth. Top producers are bold. Top producers are willing to make mistakes and to learn from these mistakes. Top producers engage fearlessly in marketing themselves to the strongest vendors and end-users. Stepping out onto the financing and leasing stage requires preparation and confidence. There is no room for tentative approaches.

You can help to shape future trends by being valuable contributors to your company, clients, and business partners. By taking responsibility for your actions and innovative ideas, you are affirming your commitment to success. Take "credit where credit is due."

Stamp Your Name on Your Next Initiative

"Claim Responsibility"
Call to Action Questions:

1) Do you take responsibility for your successes and failures?

2) Describe a success you shared with your clients. What was their reaction?

3) Describe a change in your marketing strategy because of a failed attempt. What were the lessons learned?

4) When do you place yourself in the spotlight? What are the outcomes?

5) How do you stamp your name on new initiatives?

The Best of the Best

Commercial equipment leasing and finance originators are the cornerstone of the industry. It is the originator who starts the process; the originator is the front line for every lessor, bank, or originating company. It is the responsibility of every originator to advocate for his success, the company's success, and the success of the industry. Therefore, first and foremost, originators accept the responsibility to be rainmakers, to seek out new opportunities, and to offer the very best services.

The most successful originators are financial advisors, who provide essential solutions.

A superficial, commodity-based approach does not promote excellence. The strongest originators dig deeper into every relationship and take the time to fully understand every lessee, vendor, and transaction.

It is important for you to perform at your highest level of competency every day, because so much depends upon your ability to consistently generate strong opportunities. As a knowledgeable professional, take every opportunity to flaunt your expertise, the benefits of your products, and your ability to offer viable solutions.

Be a Strong Foundation

"The Best of the Best"
<u>*Call to Action Questions:*</u>

1) Do you offer the best to every client?

2) Are you focused on those transactions and relationships you can serve the best?

3) Do you embrace strong competition and do competitive situations encourage you to perform better?

4) Do your competitors know you because of your strengths in the market?

5) Do you attract those transactions that align with your capabilities? Why? Or why not?

About the Author

Scott A. Wheeler, CLFP has been active in the commercial equipment leasing/financing industry since 1982. Scott is an accomplished senior leasing executive with extensive experience in marketing and operations. Wheeler Business Consulting LLC provides consultative services to lessors, banks, origination firms, and investors in the commercial equipment leasing/finance industry. Prior to starting Wheeler Business Consulting, Scott held executive positions with publicly held bank leasing operations and privately held independent lessors.

Scott is a current member of the Equipment Leasing & Finance Association (ELFA) and the National Equipment Finance Association (NEFA). He is a Certified Lease & Finance Professional (CLFP).

Scott is an advocate for the industry and assists professionals and organizations to reach a higher level of production and penetration in the market. Scott has an MBA from the Sellinger School of Business - Loyola University of Maryland.

Comments, suggestions or requests to be added to our weekly "Sales Tips" distribution list may be forwarded to: scott@wheelerbusinessconsulting.com.

**WHEELER BUSINESS
CONSULTING**

A portion of the proceeds from this book will be donated to the Chris Walker Education Fund.

Chris Walker was an active member and advocate of the commercial equipment leasing and finance industry. When Chris passed away in 2011, many industry professionals wanted some way they could make a donation to honor and continue Chris' great service to the industry, resulting in the creation of the Chris Walker Education Fund.

Wheeler Business Consulting is proud to support the Fund and professionals in the industry seeking additional educational opportunities.

To find out more about the Chris Walker Education Fund, how you can contribute to the Fund, or to apply for educational financial assistance provided by the Fund visit: http://www.nefassociation.org/donations/fund.asp?id=10120

Made in the USA
San Bernardino, CA
19 September 2017